Dear Annie, I Hate You

Samantha Ipema

methuen | drama

LONDON • NEW YORK • OXFORD • NEW DELHI • SYDNEY

METHUEN DRAMA
Bloomsbury Publishing Plc, 50 Bedford Square, London, WC1B 3DP, UK
Bloomsbury Publishing Inc, 1359 Broadway, New York, NY 10018, USA
Bloomsbury Publishing Ireland, 29 Earlsfort Terrace, Dublin 2, D02 AY28, Ireland

BLOOMSBURY, METHUEN DRAMA and the Methuen
Drama logo are trademarks of Bloomsbury Publishing Plc

First published in Great Britain 2025

Cover design: Holly Capper
Photography by Charlie Flint
Photography Artwork by Joe Bottomley at Pyjama Media

A catalogue record for this book is available from the British Library.

Library of Congress Control Number: 2025943242

ISBN: PB: 978-1-3505-9967-3
         ePDF: 978-1-3505-9968-0
         eBook: 978-1-3505-9969-7

Series: Modern Plays

Typeset by Westchester Publishing Services
Printed and bound in Great Britain

For product safety related questions contact productsafety@bloomsbury.com.

To find out more about our authors and books visit
www.bloomsbury.com and sign up for our newsletters.

Dear Annie, I Hate You

Samantha Ipema

Dear Annie, I Hate You

a new play by Samantha Ipema

The following text preserves the play as it was originally written. Revisions made during the rehearsal and staging processes are not reflected in this publication. As a result, the staged production may have differed.

Dear Annie, I Hate You is produced by Wild Geese Productions in association with HFH Productions.

This iteration was first performed at Riverside Studios on 8th May 2025 and transferred to Pleasance Courtyard, Edinburgh Fringe, on 30th July 2025.

Cast

Sam	**Samantha Ipema**
Annie	**Eleanor House**
Brendan	

The roles of the following characters are pre-recorded and appear throughout the show:

Mom	**Robin Ipema**
Dad	**Ben Ipema**
Micah	**Micah Ipema**
Doctor	**Dan Vryhof**
Paige	**Keegan Carr**
Laney	**Caitlin Mallory**
Courtney	**Emily Rule**
Jessie	**Kensey Berry**
Chad	**Gabriel Murphy**
Ester	**Eleanor Dunlop**

Creative Team

Creator and Writer	**Samantha Ipema**
Director and Original Dramaturg	**James Meteyard**

Associate Director for Edinburgh Fringe	**Hannah Sands**
Set and Lighting Designer	**Hugo Dodsworth**
Sound Designer	**Dan Balfour**
Co-Video Designer	**Douglas Coghlan**
Co-Video Designer	**Dan Light**
Costume Designer	**Hazel McIntosh**
Movement Director	**Jade Hackett**
Fight and Intimacy Director	**Robin Hellier**
Associate Fight and Intimacy Director	**Bethan Clark**
Development Dramaturg	**Alice Wordsworth**

The Riverside production was created with dramaturgical support and collaboration from Dan Balfour and James Meteyard.

Lead Producer	**Sarah Chamberlain of Wild Geese Productions**
Producer	**Sam Ipema of Wild Geese Productions**
Associate Producer	**Hannah Farley-Hills of HFH Productions**

Production Team

Production Manager	**Tina Dézart**
Stage Manager	**Laura Thomas**
Sound Operator	**Eliot Allison**
Dresser	**Darian Fagance**

PR Support for Riverside Studios and Edinburgh Fringe 2025	**Chloé Nelkin Consulting**
Marketing Support for Riverside Studios	**Maidwell Marketing**

Wild Geese Productions

Wild Geese Productions is an award-winning multi-platform production company with a proclivity for the absurd. Our focus is to create quirky yet thought-provoking work that centres around social issues and dynamics, told via an imaginative lens. Our aim is to uplift and unite new audiences together with stories that showcase the wonder, terror, humour and heartbreaking beauty of the human existence. Founded by Sam Ipema in 2023 with Sarah Chamberlain joining the team in 2024.

Dear Annie, I Hate You is Wild Geese Productions' theatrical debut.

www.wildgeese-productions.com/

HFH Productions

HFH Productions is an award-winning production company run by UK-based indie theatre producer, Hannah Farley-Hills. The company develops, mounts and tours theatrical productions nationally and internationally, showcasing drama and new writing that is bold, actively challenging and memorable.

Recent credits include: *Dear Annie, I Hate You* (Riverside Studios as associate to Wild Geese Productions), *Bacon* (Soho Playhouse, New York and YES24, Seoul transfer), *Flicker* (Pleasance, Edinburgh Fringe), *Surrender* (Summerhall, Arcola Theatre), *Bacon* (Summerhall, Riverside Studios, Bristol Old Vic), *Dark Noon* (Pleasance, Edinburgh Fringe for Glynis Henderson Productions), *The Naughty Fox & . . . If We've Never Been To The Moon?* (UK Tour).

www.hfh.productions/

Author's Note

This piece began in 2019, in a cramped 98-square-foot apartment I couldn't afford on the Upper West Side of New York. I was busy, burned out, and in need of a topic for an assignment at drama school at Stella Adler Studio. I figured sharing my personal trauma about having a brain aneurysm – framed as a darkly funny stand-up set where I brought her to life as a deranged, adult version of Little Orphan Annie – might be just the key to scoring an easy A.

Admittedly, turning my aneurysm into both a terrifying Orphan Annie knock-off *and* the voice inside my head was probably a bit much in hindsight, even for me. But in that small black box theatre, with my 30 teachers and peers, *Dear Annie, I Hate You* was born.

The road itself has been long and winding. Not just the reality of surviving the events the play depicts, but the reckonings it has brought me on and towards in all these years since. It certainly hasn't been linear. And it certainly hasn't been smooth. But it has led to extraordinary joys, a career I would have never imagined, and most importantly – a return back to myself.

To the missed turns, the strange detours, and all the people that brought me here – and *there are many* – I look to you. It wasn't easy. But I like to hope it was worth it. And I always, always will be indebted to you for coming on the journey.

To anyone arriving for the first, second or twenty-seventh time, I offer this:

You don't have to be a superhero to exist. You just have to live.

And if you don't know how to do that yet . . . what an exhilarating place to begin.

(And playing pretend is cool. Don't let anyone tell you it isn't.)

A Final Note

*The day I found out this piece had been approved for publication,
I got a message from my doctors with an update from my latest scan:
the inoperable aneurysm had not only remained stable – it was gone.
Which, for those not as familiar with terminal diagnoses, that isn't
something they typically do . . . ever.*

Maybe there's the science for the sequel.

With Special Thanks To . . .

Ben and Robin Ipema – for never leaving my side, nor this piece. And for being in it, before you knew you'd agreed to.

Alex Page – for being the best friend in the world that a girl could ever ask for and who I would not be here without.

Jayme Fleckenstein – who I would not be the same self without and who understands this piece more than even me.

Jordan Holden – who I would also not be the same self without and who Annie's inspiration is drawn largely out of.

Micah Ipema – for being there, always.

Eleanor House – for bringing this character to life in every way I could imagine. There is no one else I'd rather share this piece and that stage with.

James Meteyard – for being the truest partner in this from the moment you were brought on.

Dan Balfour – for pouring your love and soul into this piece when you had no reason to, and for being a truly wonderful friend.

Hugo Dodsworth – for joining and sticking on this ride despite the many meltdowns you've sat across the table for.

Douglas Coghlan – for the many, many laughs.

Dan Light – for a new and wonderful friend.

Jade Hackett – for all the goofy, wonderful light and depth you brought to this and to everywhere you touch.

Sarah Chamberlain – for being calm to my chaos and chaos to my calm.

Hannah Farley-Hills – for everything you are and jumping in head first and not looking back.

Robin Hellier and Bethan Clark – for the light and the joy that you both are.

Hazel McIntosch – for making us look cooler than we are and playing the ultimate 'cool girl' out there.

Beatrice Galloway – for whom this first iteration would have never had a chance of existing without.

Laura Thomas – for being the queen you are.

Emily Rule and Keegan Carr – for reading this script at any hour of the day or night . . . and for that one night.

Caitlin Mallory, Gabriel Murphy, Eleanour Dunlop, Kensey Berry – for answering my random message on a Tuesday night and bringing these characters to life in the best way possible.

Dan Vryhof (and Nick Vryhof) – for taking the time between shifts at the real hospital to film for my pretend one.

Chelsea Austin – for being a badass of the law.

My Friends Back Home – for being my reason I do this weird career.

My Friends In New York – for supporting me on this piece while I was still figuring out what it wanted to be.

My Friends from Central – for your constant support and encouragement.

My Friends from Stella Adler – for being the real OGs.

Pete McElligott – for being the first to take me and this crazy idea on.

Lisa Bellomo – for believing in the piece at a time no one else did.

Lee Griffifths – for sprinting through Edinburgh for me.

Carl Pasbjerg – for all your support and encouragement, even before I realized I was allowed to ask for it.

Lil Lambley – for the badass you are.

Rhys Williamson – for your enthusiasm and believing in the vision.

Chris Davies – for all the support.

Alice Wordsworth – for fearlessly diving into this leg of the race with me.

Georgina Carter and Mia Squire – for the best PR squad a girl could ask for.

All the staff at Riverside Studios, ZOO Playground, Pleasance Theatre, the rest of my friends and family, and the many, many others that have invested in getting the piece to this place.

And to Annie, for bringing me to hell and back just to prove that this was the life I was always meant to live, and preventing me from another I never would have survived in.

Dear Annie, I Hate You

For Micah.
You're Batman.

Scene 1. Science

The stage is dark. A large white curtain stands in the centre, severing the stage in half. Five spotlights shine. One across the central nervous system (ie. the central platform from which all other production elements stem). The other four spread across each white plinth scattered to the left and right of the central platform. Atop each of the four plinths sits a CRT TV from the '90s.

A '90s-style camcorder sits in the center of the plinth. **Sam** *(20–30s) sits on the side in the audience, staring at the camcorder in deep contemplation. Once the audience is seated,* **Sam** *stands up and approaches the camcorder on the central plinth.*

Even more memories topple over each other across the screens. She gently picks up the camcorder.

Right as she is about to speak, **Annie** *(20–30s) arrives as a late audience member and sits in the vacant seat.* **Sam** *pauses. Then, begins.*

Sam   86 billion neurons. That is what a typical brain is composed of. A network of 86 billion neurons that fires millions of signals in simultaneous succession to complete a simple action . . . Lifting your knee . . . straightening your leg . . . taking a step.

She gently sets down the camcorder and steps off the platform.

There are a lot of things we still don't understand about this three-pound piece of gray and white matter floating around inside of our heads. But we do know this –

She reaches into the platform and pulls out a long light cable.

The wiring of this 86-billion wide firing squad – unique to every individual – shapes every single one of our thoughts, beliefs, and personality traits. These pathways decide how we respond to all the events in our lives . . .

Sam *plugs in the first cable to the far USL plinth. The CRT TV atop it starts to play silent recordings from her early childhood.*

I am by no means an expert or a studied neurologist, by the way. I've just spent a fair time learning about the brain at this point in life . . . but more on that later.

She pulls out a second cable.

With every event, we either create new or affirm old neural pathways. These pathways are necessary to our development – learning how to walk, talk, and form new connections as we go through life . . . Hey there.

She winks at an audience member as she plugs the second cable into the USR plinth. More childhood memories turn on.

Our neurons then scatter fragments of information from these events across different regions of the brain to store and be called upon later. But when we re-*call*, or re-*member*, these fragments . . .

Sam *plugs in the third neuron and returns to the central platform.*

Our brain fills in the gaps, in order to create a cohesive narrative of what probably happened. We do this for survival . . . To make sense of the past. In order to predict the future. To inform the present moment.

This is where stories come from.

The brain doesn't aim for accuracy though. It doesn't pull up a perfect replay of these events. It aims for coherence, because coherence gives us a sense of understanding, a sense of safety . . . a sense of control.

She steps off and pulls out the final neuron cable.

But there are many things that can influence the rewiring of these pathways over time. And the biggest one – the cause for the most significant amount of change to these neural pathways – is a life-altering experience. Those key moments . . . That light up when you think about them . . .

That changed the trajectory of your life and pinged you into all sorts of unexpected directions . . .

The moments that change you. Where your whole life changes right in front of you.

She plugs in the final cable. Even more memories toppling over one another alight the screens. A beat. She gently picks up the camcorder.

This story begins the first time that I knew my life was about to change. The day I met my big brother Micah.

She presses 'Play'.

Scene 2. Growing Up, Part 1

Memories of her and her adopted brother **Micah** *fill the screens as she flies to the far USL TV.*

Sam He'd been picked up and flown all the way across the ocean from South Korea to our little town in Kalamazoo, Michigan.

I was three. He was four.

He ran away from my parents in the airport. And he bit my babysitter. I knew instantly we were going to get along.

When our brains register that a significant event is about to happen – a neural signal is sent to key sensory organs and a chemical is released. In this case – dopamine. Preparing the body to *pay attention*. Something *exciting* is *about to happen*. But when he walked in, all I remember seeing were the biggest, roundest glasses that took up half his face and the wickedest lopsided smile I had ever seen.

My parents explained to me that Micah's brain worked a little bit differently than mine. That he was older than me. But it might take him longer to understand things because –

Mom *(40–50s) pops up on the center USR screen as* **Sam** *sits, childlike, opposite of her.*

Mom He has something called Down's Syndrome, honey.

Sam So it was important that –

Sam *spins around and now* **Dad** *(40–50s) pops up on the center USL screen.*

Dad You need to be extra kind and extra patient with him, sweetie –

She spins back to the audience at center.

Sam   And all I remember thinking was that I didn't care . . . Because I'd just met my new best friend.

Sam *jumps up. A song like 'American Pie' or something reminiscent of warm '90s nostalgia plays at full blast. All the TVs play with memories together while a life-sized silhouette of* **Micah** *(20s) is projected onto the back curtain. The two begin to play.*

Sam   We grew up attached at the hip! Living with Micah is like living in a *fantasy* because he sees life so differently. To him, there is no difference between fact or fiction. So if a superhero exists in a story, it means they must exist in reality.

Or even, that they must exist in this room right here among us . . .

(To audience members) I'm looking at you.

Or actually . . . that *we* must be the superhero right here among us!

So our lives were filled with adventure. Undercover spies! Pirate expeditions! Space explorations! And so many, *so* many . . . superhero battles. *Batman*, particularly. Which I didn't – and I still don't – agree with because he has no *real* superpowers. But that didn't – and *still* doesn't – matter to Micah.

The music shifts to a superhero-like theme song. **Sam** *and* **Micah** *take it very seriously.*

Batman and Robin had very important things to do and places to be every day. We had mysteries to solve. Crooks to capture. Gadgets to assemble. Plots to foil. Bombs to defuse. People to rescue – And of course, the most important superhero mission of all . . . Go on business trips. Because that's what Dad did.

Micah *(smiling/cool)*   *Business.*

The two smile.

Sam   And then I went to school.

Sam's *friends suddenly pop up on every screen.* **Paige**, **Laney**, **Jessie**, *and* **Courtney** *all appear.*

Paige (*annoyed*)   What're we doing here? Why are you carrying a briefcase?

Laney (*disgusted*)   My mom told me not to touch people. They're dirty.

Jessie (*through tears*)   I'm Jessie, I don't want to be here.

Courtney (*confident*)   I'm Courtney. I like your butterfly clips.

Sam   . . . and life changed.

Scene 3. Growing Up, Part 2

The friends appear faster, more confident, and slightly older now. Certain of who they are and their places within the world.

Paige   Did you see what Ryan posted on my MySpace last night?

Laney   My mom says MySpace is where creepy guys live.

Jessie (*whining*)   I have to use my brother's MySpace because I don't have a computer.

Courtney   His profile pic is lame, Paige, you can do way better.

Jessie   MySpace is scary.

Sam (*trying to keep up*)   Wait, guys, what's MySpace?

Two gasp, two giggle out of embarrassment.

Paige   Omg. What?

Courtney   You don't know what MySpace is?!

Jessie   That's so sad for you . . .

Laney (*disgusted*)   What do you do? You don't still play pretend do you?

Sam (*overwhelmed*)   No!

Long silence as they wait . . .

Sam *turns back to the audience defensively.*

Our brains register social rejection as a literal threat to our survival. So being *'cool'* isn't just a desire, it is a neurobiological survival system that says 'good job, you're staying alive'. The prefrontal cortex isn't fully developed in adolescence, so logic doesn't override the emotional urgency of fitting in and I didn't realize that apparently other people didn't go on superhero battles anymore, that

that wasn't *cool*! So I *separated* from Micah. Told him to go find his own friends because I found mine. And I filled my life with other things.

The friends all pop up again on the screens and smile.

Paige   Wanna go to the mall?

Sam   Normal things.

Courtney   Wanna go to the beach?

Sam   Things that normal people do.

Laney   You should really date Brendan.

Jessie (*swooning*)   He really likes you.

Brendan *pops on the screen, but the image is blurred. Over the top it reads. '***Brendan** *did not consent to the use of this footage.'*

Brendan   Uh, yeah, I guess, uh . . . do you wanna go out with me?

Sam   . . . Sure?

Dinggggg!

All (*squealing*)   Ohhhhmyyyygoooddddddddd!

Sam (*confidently*)   So I learned how to mall, I learned how to beach, and I learned how to flirt with people . . .

(*to audience member*) Hey, what's your name?

(*if no answer*) . . . Seriously, what's your name?

Audience Member *either responds with their name or doesn't.*

Sam   Whatever. Mind if I call you gorgeous?

Dinggggg!

All (*squealing*)   Eeeeeeeeekk!!! They are gorgeousssss!!!!

Sam *spins and steps off the plinth, overly-confident now. Trying to impress the audience.*

Sam   And all the while, I learned how to *school*. I figured out how to diagram a sentence . . . Which is to break down a sentence . . . Which is something I've never had to use again until this moment right here. I figured out how to point to Albuquerque on a map . . . which is . . . not important right now! And I figured out how to do multiplication, in rhombus shapes, that made my brain hurt. So I went home and I complained to my mom about it. She told me –

Mom *appears on USL TV.*

Mom   It's okay, honey. You're not book smart, you're other smart.

Sam *stares, confused.*

Sam   I started to wonder what that meant. So I complained to my dad about it. His solution? Sit me down for five hours and tell me the history of the rhombus.

Dad *appears on the USR TV.*

Dad   There is no history of a rhombus actually, honey, the term 'rhombus' actually comes from the Greek word 'rhombi', so think of a square –

Sam *rolls her eyes and cuts him off.*

Sam   Thank you, Dad! Then I got older and life changed again. I realized apparently people were smarter than me . . .

The friends pop back up on various TVs again.

Paige   What did everyone get on their SATs? I got a 36P.

Sam   Better at things than me.

Laney   Just remember the plan is for everyone to meet at 12pm at south beach –

Sam *trips and it's funny.*

Sam   But that I was relatively funny? Maybe that could be my thing?

Laney   Hahahaha! You're so funny Sam!

Jessie   You're hilarious!

Paige   It's not like what you say, but what you do.

Courtney   It's just in the way you act, you just naturally are.

Sam *grabs the balloon from atop the central left TV and treks on.*

Sam   But that wasn't enough of a thing, okay? And I needed to find one. And I tried a lot of them. Singing? Micah told me –

Micah   It's not good Sam.

Sam   Cheerleading?

Paige   You're just not built for it.

Courtney   If it makes you happy you should do it!

Laney   Maybe you could be the base of the pyramid?!

Jessie (*whining*)   I wish I was as tall as you, then I could eat whatever I want.

Sam   And we already established that –

Mom (*attempting to comfort*)   You're not book smart, honey, you're other smart.

Sam   So I started to feel like I wasn't ever going to find it. My thing. My calling. My *je ne sais quoi*. Until one day . . . the world slowed down. Everything stopped. And nothing mattered anymore. Because I started falling in love for the first time.

She blows up and reveals the soccer ball balloon.

With soccer.

Celine Dion's 'It's All Coming Back To Me Now' or something similar plays.

Now, what happens neurologically when we fall in love is that the brain releases – actually, who gives a shit what's happening neurologically? Birds start chirping. Music from every love song ever starts playing. It makes no sense and it feels fucking amazing.

She stares lovingly at the soccer balloon as they begin a meet-cute montage.

When soccer and I first met, I knew instantly it was going to be a life-long love affair. We fell hard and we fell fast for one another, and soon every moment was about being together. Rain . . . shine . . . anytime life changed, it didn't matter. She was always there for me.

Beat.

A whistle blows.

Sam *looks up, suddenly serious.*

Scene 4. Soccer Game

Sam   It's March 1st, 2015.

I'm in my third year of university and I still haven't found what my thing is.

All my other friends have.

Paige is a pre-med student.

Paige *pops up on the USL TV.*

Paige   I'm going to be a surgeon.

Sam   Which means she thinks she's right about everything.

Paige   That's because I am right about everything.

Sam   Of course you are, Paige! Jessie is the opposite. She's studying psychology to become a therapist.

Jessie *pops up on the USR TV as* **Sam** *passes.*

Jessie (*crying*)   I'm just, I'm really worried about him. He's probably had a really difficult, traumatic past with lots of abuse . . .

Sam   That was about a cat she saw on the street.

Laney is studying to be an Elementary school teacher, but she's really here to get her MRS degree.

Ding ding ding! **Laney** *shows off an engagement ring.*

Laney (*squealing*)   Ring by spring!

Sam   And Courtney's thing is to not care about having a thing.

Courtney   Yeah, institutions are stupid. Whatever.

Sam   Whereas I took a different approach. You can't rush greatness. Viola Davis was 43 when she got her big break.

Thomas Edison took 2,442 times to make the light bulb. And I had 3 different interviews for unpaid internships set up . . . so I was well on my way.

And to celebrate, I decided to skip class and go play with cute boys and their balls.

If the audience laughs, she reacts defensively.

Soccer balls! It was an All Men's Recreational League.

The friends pop back on unexpectedly.

Laney   Which meant she wasn't going anywhere professionally.

Sam   I was the only girl on the team!

Paige   That's because you saw the sign-up sheet and your name is Sam so they let you play because they thought you were a boy –

Sam   It doesn't matter, we were in the finals –!

Jessie/Courtney   Of a Division 4 league.

Sam   Are you on my side or not?!

Courtney   Yeahhhh!

Laney   We're all here for you!!

Paige   Lol so sensitive!

Jessie   She'd just broken up with Brendan, she was going through a lot.

Sam *shoots a look at them.*

Sam   There wasn't a good women's league. So, I was playing with Nick. And all of his very sexy friends.

A sexy, popular, early 2010s song like Ginuwine's 'Riding My Pony' starts to play. **Sam** *grabs the camcorder off the plinth.*

Now, this is important. Nick is one of those guys . . . Where did you go? I just – . . . ah, there you are!

She spots an audience member towards the front now deemed as **'Nick'**. *The camcorder broadcasts an image of him/her on either the large curtain or TVs.*

Nicholas is one of those guys that you first meet and think – 'You're such a douchebag. There is no way we're ever going to be friends.' But then you sit and talk to him . . . and you get to know him . . . and you realize . . . 'you are a douchebag, and there's no way we're ever going to be friends.'

And then we became best –

She laughs and stops.

Well, it was a bit . . .

We had both just broken up with our –

You know what? It doesn't matter.

We were best friends.

Anyways!

She runs away and tells the audience member playing '**Nick**' *to hold onto the camcorder.*

I was standing in my gear, arguing with another guy who was convinced I couldn't play 'because I was a girl and I was going to get hurt', when Nick came up to dissolve the situation by slapping me on the back and saying 'it's okay, dude, she's basically just a dude anyways.'

Beat.

And something.

Inside of me.

Shifted.

Another beat. She walks slowly back to **Nick**.

I am not a dude.

I am a hot, funny, somewhat popular girl.

Who is also *really good at soccer.*

*An **Announcer**'s voice echoes across the stage. Suddenly, we're inside the most epic recreational league championship game of all time. **Sam** gently takes the camcorder from **Nick**, posing together for a quick video before placing it on the USR TV.*

Announcer   LADIES AND GENTLEMEN WELCOME BACK TO THE ALL MEN'S RECREATIONAL LEAGUE DIVISION FOUR FINAL WHERE TWO TEAMS FACE OFF TO WIN THE GRAND PRIZE OF A T-SHIRT.

Sam *steps up on the platform.*

Announcer   SAM STEPS UP FOR THE KICKOFF. HEAD TO HEAD WITH THE 'DON'T GET HURT GUY'. SHE IS THE ONLY FEMALE ON THE MEN'S LEAGUE. WOW, HOW AMAZING IS THAT.

Laney (*screaming*)   You're amazing!!

Courtney   Kick their ass!

Paige   You look very sexy –

Jessie   – and cool, Sam!!

Announcer   THE CROWD IS EMPHATIC. REFEREE BLOWS HIS WHISTLE. AND THE GAME STARTS.

*A song begins to play. **Sam** 'kicks off' the balloon and begins to run.*

Friends (*squealing*)   OMG you're so amazing!! Aaahhhhhh!!!

Chad   Hot.

Announcer   THEY KEEP CONTROL IN THE MIDFIELD. SAM FINDS HERSELF SPACE ON THE RIGHT WING. SHE CALLS FOR THE BALL.

In slow motion, **Sam** *mimes calling for the ball and winning it.*

Announcer   AND A WORLD-CLASS FIRST TOUCH.
THE FOOTWORK IS AMAZING. SHE GOES AROUND
1, AROUND 2 – SHE SPLITS THE DEFENSE WITH A
PERFECT PASS TO THE LEFT WING. A BEAUTIFUL
SPACE OPENS UP IN FRONT OF THE GOAL. NOW
IS HER TIME TO SHINE. SHE'S SHOULDER TO
SHOULDER WITH THE 'DON'T GET HURT' GUY.
THEY ENTER THE BOX . . . THIS IS GONNA BE A
STICKY ONE, FOLKS.

Friends (*screaming*)   Wooooo!!! Kick his ass, Sam!!!

Announcer   SHE LOOKS AT NICK AND HIS SEXY
FRIENDS AND MAKES SURE THEY'RE WATCHING.

Sam *eyes '***Nick***'.*

Chad   She's so cool, man. Super underrated.

Sam   Thanks! I know!

Announcer   HER UNIMPORTANT MALE TEAMMATE
DOES AN AVERAGE CROSS FROM THE LEFT
SIDE – BUT SAM MAKES IT WORK AS SHE LEAPS
INTO THE AIR! THE 'DON'T GET HURT GUY' IS
CONFUSED AND LOST. COMPLETELY DEFEATED BY
IPEMA'S INCREDIBLE SKILL. THE BALL IS FLYING
THROUGH THE AIR AT A SHOCKING SPEED –

The screech of a megaphone. A loud sigh. A **New Announcer**
takes over. **Sam** *pauses her slow motion leap and breaks character
momentarily. Looks into the lights, confused.*

New Announcer/Annie   AND JUST AT THAT MOMENT,
SAM LOOKS TO HER RIGHT AND NOTICES HER EX –
BRENDAN – AND THINKS 'WHAT THE HELL ARE
YOU DOING HERE? WE JUST BROKE UP –'

Sam *shoots a daggered glance to* **Annie** *as* **Annie** *lifts a hand and
flicks it.*

WHAM.

A loud sound of a ball finding its mark as **Sam** *is forcibly knocked onto the platform.*

Lights out.

Scene 5. Diagnosis

Videos click on the TV sets to a doctor's office. **Doc** *appears on the first screen.*

Doc   Hi Sam.

Sam (*confused*)   Hi?

Doc   How are you today?

Sam (*catching up*)   Uh – Fine?

Doc   Do you know why you're here?

Sam   I think so?

Doc   Great.

Sam   Wait. No. Sorry. Can you tell me?

Doc   Are your parents here? Your parents should really be here for this.

The screens momentarily go dark. Scene replays. The **Doc** *and* **Sam**'s *parents now fill the screens.*

Doc (*same as before*)   Hi Sam.

Sam   Hi.

Doc   Are these your parents?

Sam   Yes.

Mom   Hi. Yes. I'm Sam's mom. I'm incredibly anxious.

Doc   Hi, nice to meet you Mom.

Dad   Hi, I'm Sam's dad. I'd like to get a second opinion.

Sam   Dad!

Doc   Hi. Of course. Great to meet you, dad. Shall we get star –

Mom   Honey, don't you think Brendan should be here –?

Sam   Huh? Uh, su –

Scene replays. **Doc**, **Mom**, **Dad**, *and* **Brendan** *fill the screens now.*

Doc   Hi Sam.

Sam (*confused*)   Hi.

Doc   Is this everyone?

Mom   Hello.

Dad   Hi.

Brendan   Hi, I'm Brendan. I'm Sam's boyfriend.

Sam   Ex-boyfriend.

Brendan   It's complicated. Nice to meet you.

Doc   Great. Shall we get started?

Everyone grunts in approval.

Mom   Oh my gosh. We forgot about Micah.

Sam *groans. The scene replays once more. Faster. Everyone popping on different screens.*

Doc (*exhausted*)   Alright. Everyone here?

Dad   Yup.

Mom   Yes.

Brendan   Yep!

Micah   I am Batman.

Sam *sighs.*

Doc   Right. So Sam . . . You've been hit in the head.

Sam   Right.

Doc   Everything seemed fine initially.

Doc's *voice starts becoming inaudible.*

Sam   Okay.

Doc   But then we took a second look . . .

Sam   Mhmm.

Doc   Found a spot . . .

His voice sounds almost completely underwater now. Unintelligible.

Sam   Okay.

Doc (*inaudible*)   Noticed – something . . . un – unusual – . . . on . . . – scan.

Sam   . . . Right.

Doc (*inaudible*)   Do you – know – what a——is –?

Sam   Uh . . .

Recording cuts out. **Sam** *stares for a long moment. Then continues.*

Sam   When our brain registers that a negative event is about to happen, it releases a chemical. Cortisol. Preparing the body to pay attention. Something threatening is about to happen. People often describe it as a trap-door feeling. But to me, it felt like my life had suddenly slowed down and plunged underwater . . .

It happened when I got the call earlier that day . . . That was the moment I knew my life was about to change permanently . . .

Annie *groans loudly from the audience. The recording of the* **Nurse**'s *voicemail plays. But it's tin-like. Underwater. Cutting out periodically.*

Nurse   Hi Sam . . . this is Nurse Jackson. Metro Health hospital. We. . . . We took another look and found something on your scan. We'd . . . like you to come back in for a second opinion. Please call us back. The moment you get this message. Talk soon.

The phone clicks. **Sam** *stands completely still. A silence stretches for too long. Behind her, a gray, water-like world begins to fill the curtains behind her. Bits flaking apart in slow-motion. Like reflections coming from inside her mind.*

Sam (*contemplating*)   . . . I think if you watch carefully in these moments, you can actually see the walls starting to flake apart and the pillars of your old life – your old reality – starting to crumble. I think there's actually something beautiful about it . . . Terrible. Awful. But, beautiful . . . Because in a weird way, nothing is ever clearer than in these moments. Everything that is ahead of you. Everything is behind you. And you . . . suspended. Right there in the middle of it with a choice to make.

She snaps out of the reflection, remembering where she is. Back to 'performing'.

Sorry. Uh, I didn't go in right after the game. I actually waited a few days before I did . . . I had an interview later that day and I –

Annie   For fuck's sake.

Annie *groans and stands up. Annoyed and fed up. She stares at* **Sam** *as she loudly gathers her things and stomps out of the room through the wrong door. Shuffling can be heard backstage.* **Sam** *onstage panics, but tries to continue on as planned.*

(*To audience*)   Uh . . . Oh my god . . . I'm so sorry . . .

Sam *ignores and continues.*

Uh – sorry. Uh. Anyways! I wanted to prove that I was fine . . . so I, uh . . . I didn't go in – . . . but something – let's call it intuition . . . some instinct or voice in my head – started just . . . *nagging* at me . . . telling me to go in –

More shuffling is audibly heard. The curtain ruffles. **Sam** *notices but tries to speed up.*

There are no symptoms with these things, so they didn't notice anything at first. But they took another look. And that was when the Nurse called –

Suddenly, a misfired cue plays across the television screens. The starting notes of 'Space Odyssey' begins to play. The picture of a sun slowly dawning over the earth takes over the stage. **Sam** *watches in panic.*

. . . called me . . . and told me to come back in . . . and then the doctor came in . . . and sat me down . . . and told me –

Bang. The sound reaches a climax that makes **Sam** *jump. Suddenly, a trombone and drums are heard behind the curtains. Lights flashing. The set completely out of* **Sam***'s control.* **Sam** *looks to Board Operator.*

Sam   [Name of Board Operator] !

She apologizes to audience members as she runs up the steps to the tech box.

Sam   [Name of Board Operator] !!!! Go to a show stop! Go to a show stop!!

The Board Operator disconnects the power. Everything shuts down. **Sam** *freezes, awkwardly standing amongst the audience. Slightly out of breath. Trying to stay calm.*

Sam (*panicked*)   I'm so sorry.

Can we –?

(*to Board Operator*) Let's just go back a few cues.

Screens return to normal. **Sam** *looks around the crowd, uneasy.*

(*to audience*)   I'm sorry. I'm so sorry. I don't know what's . . . Um. Sorry. Anyways, that was when the doctor had sat me down and told me that I have a –

Another misfired cue. Bigger and better than ever. Every screen, light and projection taken over in a nod to the most epic opening ever. 'Space Odyssey'. The Big Bang. *But better. The sun continues to rise . . . wait, no. It's not the sun. It's* **Annie**'s *face. Smiling.*

Annie (*off-stage*)   In a world . . . where dinosaurs used to roam . . . where we all started as nothing . . . where Sam thought she was doing a one-woman show all by herself . . . and thought it was good . . .

. . . then.

. . . came.

. . . Me.

The final notes to 'Space Odyssey' play. **Annie**'s *face takes over the entire stage, God-like. Her face splits in two as the curtains pull apart. Behind them is an even more spectacular second set with double the amount of CRT TVs placed atop a jungle gym of plinths.*

Music and lights shift dramatically. A single spotlight on the top DSL plinth. **Annie** *scrambles into place. She begins to sing 'I Will Survive'.*

Sam   What the fuck.

Sam *sprints to the platform and shoves* **Annie** *out of her spotlight. Lights switch back to* **Sam**'s *set.* **Annie** *waits.*

Annie (*to Sam*)   Are you going to introduce me?

Sam (*ignoring*)   Anyways, that's when the doc –

'Say My Name' by Destiny's Child plays. **Annie** *sings. The production once again taken over by her.* **Sam** *signals the Board Operator. Production shifts back to 'normal' again.*

Sam   So, that was when the doctor –

'Oops I Did It Again' by Britney Spears plays. **Annie** *sings.* **Sam** *signals the Board Operator again. Back to normal.*

Sam   So that's when the doctor told me –

'Milkshake' by Kelis plays. **Annie** *sings and now grinds on* **Sam**. **Sam** *moves away and returns the production to normal one more time.*

Sam   So that was when the doctor sat me down and told me –!!

A slower ballad begins. 'If I Die Young' by The Band Perry. **Annie** *sings along, enjoying the chaos.* **Sam** *screams and runs at* **Annie**. *The song switches midtackle. 'Wrecking Ball' by Miley Cyrus plays.* **Annie** *sings and catches* **Sam** *in a loving embrace.*

Sam *wrestles out of the embrace.* **Annie** *winks.*

Annie   Smack my bitch up!

Sam   What?

'Smack My Bitch Up' by The Prodigy plays as **Annie** *smacks* **Sam***'s bottom. Hard.*

Sam *(yelling)*   No one even knows who you are!!

Annie *sings 'Call Me Maybe' by Carly Rae Jepsen.*

Sam   OKAY! FINE. FINE! STOP.

Annie   Are you gonna introduce me?

Sam *hesitates.* **Annie** *goes to sing another song.*

Sam   – Yes.

Okay.

Fine.

Shit.

Fine.

Shit.

Okay.

There's someone you should all probably meet.

This is Annie . . .

My brain aneurysm.

Annie   Hi! So nice to meet you. Oh. What's your name? Gorgeous?

Sam   ANNIE.

Sam *beckons her over to her.* **Annie** *ignores her.*

Annie   One sec. What's up?

Sam   Are you going to behave?

Annie   Of course!

Sam   I'm serious.

Annie (*mocking*)   Serious.

Sam   Annie.

Annie (*mocking*)   Sammy.

Sam   Okay, just –

Ugh.

Let me think.

Ugh.

Oh my god . . . where was I?

Annie *grabs the camcorder from the USR TV and points it at* **Sam**. *She presses 'record' and the production suddenly switches to an interrogation-style drama.*

Annie (*serious*)   You were about to talk about how you were sad.

Sam   Right, thank you.

Annie   How your parents seemed sad and you were really sad –

Sam   Thank you, Annie.

Annie   How when you looked at Micah's face, it made you really –

Sam   Okay, I got it Annie. Thank you so much. Give me that.

Sam *grabs the camcorder and hits 'stop'. Production resumes to normal.* **Sam** *smiles.*

Sam   So that was when the doctor sat me down and told me I had a brain aneurysm –

Annie   – Which is great.

Beat.

Sam   *Which is* a really annoying little balloon filled with blood stemming off the central artery inside my head.

Annie   Which only 1 in a billion people have.

Sam   That's not true. About 1 in 100,000 people are affected by them.

Annie   Still really rare.

Beat.

Sam   Anyways! The doctors say they don't know where they come from. They just appear out of nowhere. Without any symptoms –

Annie (*winking*)   Some people would call me an enigma.

Sam   – and then they just sit there. Waiting. Like a bomb that could go off at moment without warning.

Annie   BAM! Just kidding. Not yet.

Sam   Annie!

Annie (*not sorry*)   Sorry.

Beat. Faster now.

Sam   The hit from the soccer ball hadn't caused Annie to appear, by the way –

Annie   I'd been there all along.

Sam   Annie . . .

Annie   Sleeping.

Sam   Please . . .

Annie   Waiting.

Sam   Either way, she was very present now! And that day, I had a choice to make. I could either get a life-saving –

Annie   But potentially life-ending . . .

Sam   – *surgery* to get *rid* of her. Or I could choose to live with . . . *this* . . . for the *rest* of my life.

Annie   You're welcome.

Sam   *Forever*.

Annie   Lucky you!

Sam   Never knowing whether she would go off.

Annie   BANG!

Sam (*snapping*)   Get off. OFF! Off my stage. I'm going to the next scene. Go.

Annie (*fake offended*)   Sheeeeshh. Ohhhkayyyyy!

Oh wait . . .

Scene change!

Annie *does a 'scene change' gesture. The production goes momentarily berserk. Her smiling face flashing on all of the screens.* **Sam** *waits patiently.*

Sam   Once I –

The production kicks off again. **Annie**'s *face reappeared.* **Sam**
*tries to start again. The production goes berserk again . . . and
again . . . and again. Until finally –*

Sam   Once I found out about Annie the doctor left to give
us some space!

(*sighs*) Nobody spoke for ages. I think we were afraid to. If
anyone spoke that would break the spell and it would all
suddenly be real. But when I looked at my parents squished
together in the same tiny waiting-room chair, I –

She chuckles. Then stops. Her voice catches.

They'd never looked small before. My mom's little pale
white hand was silently clutching my dad's trouser leg. They
seemed old, worn down, for the first time ever and I – . . .
Well, I start to feel a hand slowly start to slither up my
shoulder. *Brendan!*

She shouts at **Brendan** *and removes his imagined hand.*

Eventually somebody was going to have to speak. It was
getting ridiculous. And I felt like we could all use a joke to
lighten up the room so I –

*She looks around. Hesitates. Looks around again. Hesitates.
Leans back.*

'And here I thought the worst thing I'd have to tell you
today was that Brendan and I broke up again!'

All the faces on the screens look at her, incredibly dismayed.

Chaos ensues. Mom starts laugh-sobbing . . .

Mom (*laugh-sobbing*)   That is not funny Sam.

Sam   Dad starts comforting Mom –

Dad   It's okay, honey, she's just using jokes because she
doesn't know how to deal with it.

Sam   Brendan chimes in, unhelpfully.

Brendan   I mean, we're not really broken up. It's more of a 'taking a break' situation I'd say.

Sam   And then the Doc –

Doc   So Sam, have you had a chance to think about –

Mom   Why wouldn't you say anything to me about it? I thought we were close?

Dad   It's not a reflection of you, honey, I'm sure she was going to –

Doc   I can give everyone a bit more sp –

Mom   No, it's okay, we're fine.

Dad   We're ready to talk about it.

Micah   . . . I need bathroom.

Mom/Dad   Micah, not now!!!

Breath.

Sam   And that was when the questions started . . . Mom starts asking questions like –

Mom   How are you feeling, honey? What are you thinking? Do you want to go home and talk about it?

Sam   Dad has more pragmatic questions like –

Dad   Are you going to go back to class today? Back to school? Home with us? Out to dinner to talk? Because we definitely need to talk more about this.

Sam   Thanks, Dad. I know we need to talk more about it.

But the whole time . . .

The doctor glitches on. Too many voices. A cacophony of each talking over one another builds again.

Doc   You're one of the lucky ones, Sam. Most people don't catch an Annie until it's too late.

Brendan   I can pick up your stuff, babe, or stay over
tonight if you want –

Sam *ignores everyone and stares ahead at a single TV glitching.*

Sam   . . . I just kept staring at Micah.

Pause.

You could tell from his face that he didn't know what was
going on. But he knew it was something. Something bad.
Those big round glasses glancing around the room . . . You
know, I promised him ever since we were kids I would take
care of him. So in that moment something inside of me – . . .
because – . . . So when that ridiculous little smile quirked
up at me and said –

Micah   What's wrong, Sam?

Sam   I – . . . Nothing, buddy.

Micah   Is it bad?

Sam (*shakes her head*)   No.

Micah   Are you sure?

Sam (*nods*)   I'm sure.

Micah   How do you know?

Sam (*clears her throat*)   Well, because, Micah . . . 'I'm
Batman'.

Batman *music plays. He giggles.*

Micah   *Batman!*

Sam *giggles. Then shifts.*

Sam   So I did what any superhero would do . . . and I went
to a party with my friends.

Music starts.

The production shifts into a 'College Party'.

Scene 6. Party

Sam That night wasn't just any party, okay? It was the Recreational League Championship Party at Nick's house. *Everyone* was gonna be there. And *everyone* knows that if you miss one party? You miss five parties. And you and your social life may as well be dead in a ditch already. I knew eventually I would need to talk about the – Annie – but that night I wanted to fill my life with as much noise as possible. Because everything was fine. I was going to be fine. It was all going to be fine.

Annie (*Off-stage*) It was definitely not going to be fine.

Sam Yes it was. It was definitely fine.

Annie (*Off-stage*) It was not.

Sam It was too.

Annie (*Off-stage*) Not.

Sam It was! I was. It was all . . . FINE!

A doorbell rings. College friends all suddenly fill the screens.

Paige (*squealing*) Oh my god, Sam! I can't believe you're here!

Jessie (*crying*) Omg, are you alright?

Sam Yeah I'm fine!

Courtney You want a drink?

Laney Don't offer her a drink! She probably can't have a drink – She's just had surgery!

Sam No, I haven't had surgery! And yes, I will take a drink!

Jessie (*crying*) Are you sure you want to be here?

Courtney Why wouldn't she want to be here? It's Sam.

Paige   She doesn't want to sit and cry about it all night like you, Jessie.

Sam   Yeah, no, they're right. It's fine! Guys, I'm fine! It's all going to be fine!

The music plays louder as **Sam** *struts around the party.*

By the time I walked in, everyone already knew about Annie . . . Hey, Chad.

Chad   Hey, Sam!

Sam   I'd told my roommates about it and asked them not to tell anyone . . . and obviously they told everyone . . . because why wouldn't they? They're my friends! (*grimacing*) Hey Ester.

Ester (*somberly*)   Hey, Sam.

Sam (*groaning*)   When the brain perceives someone as having something unique or special about them such as a diagnosis – hiiiii popular girl I don't know the name of . . .

Popular Girl   Hiiiiiiii.

Sam   – people tend to treat that person a little bit differently. So when I –

Record scratch. **Annie**'s *voice takes over the party speakers.*

Annie (*Off-stage*)   So what she's saying is when she walked in she was suddenly hot and cool and popular and she'd never been that before and that was all thanks to me!

Sam *pauses.*

Sam   *No*! What I'm saying is that when you're in these situations, you have a choice to make. You can cower and be miserable and tell everyone to fuck off, or you can –

Another doorbell rings. **Annie** *re-enters the stage in a pink over-the-top Batman suit.*

Annie   Or you can be the life of the party and everyone will love you for it. Let's party.

Sam   One of us has to change.

Annie   Who wears it better?

They enter the living room. Immediately met by a wave of cheers along with **Popular Girl** *on the central USR TV.*

Popular Girl   OH MY GODDD. Hiiiiiiiiiiiiiiiiii.

Sam & Annie   Oh My Goddd. Hiiiiiiiiiiiiiiii.

Popular Girl   My aunt actually had a brain tumor too.

Sam   Oh my god. It's actually not a brain tumor.

Annie   I'm a billion times more unique than a brain tumor.

Popular Girl   Oh my god. Is it contagious?

Sam (*laughing*)   Oh my god. Yeah.

Annie   Not as contagious as your stupidity.

Popular Girl (*gasps*)   Oh my god. Ew.

Sam (*uncomfortable*)   Oh my god. Just kidddinnnnngggggg.

Popular Girl   Hahaha.

Sam   Hahaha.

Annie (*mocking*)   Hahahahahaha. Let's go.

Annie *pulls* **Sam** *up and the scene jumps forward into the kitchen with* **Paige**.

Paige (*shouting*)   Hey Sam, are you having fun?

Sam   Yeah, Paige, are you?

Paige   My professor told me like 1 in 50 people have brain aneurysms.

Sam   Wow, that's crazy!

Annie   Thank you so much for that useless information, Paige!

Paige   Honestly, of all the brain surgeries this one is like the best one to get! I'm not worried!

Sam   Yeah, me neither!

Annie   You probably should be!

(*to Sam*) Are you having a good time?

Sam   Yeah, I'm having a great time.

The scene flips again, this time playing beer pong in the game room with **Ester.**

Ester (*somber*)   Hi Sammmm.

Sam (*depressed*)   Hi Ester.

Annie (*annoyed*)   Hereeee comesss the God squaddd.

Ester   We heard the news . . . How's your heart?

Sam   Oh. It's good . . . It's my head actually.

Annie   Too bad you don't have either.

Ester   I want you to know that you're in our prayers.

Sam   Thanks, Ester.

Annie   Jesus.

Ester   This can happen to anyone.

Sam   You're right, Ester.

Annie   Mother-fucking –

Ester   It's gonna be okay. God gives his toughest battles to his strongest soldiers.

Sam *and* **Annie** *look at each other.*

Sam   Thanks, Ester.

Ester   Let's pray. Dear God, who art in Heaven, hallowed by thy name, thy kingdom come, thy will be –

Annie (*to Sam*)   Are you having a good time?

Sam (*challenging*)   Yeah, I'm having a great time.

Sam *kicks the cups off and the scene flips to the dance floor with* **Courtney.**

Courtney (*shouting*)   HEY, SAM, REMEMBER THIS SONG?

Sam   YEAH –

Sam & Annie   I LOVE IT!!

Sam *shoots a look at* **Annie.** **Annie** *dances at* **Sam,** *completely unencumbered.* **Sam** *tries her best to ignore, but* **Annie** *becomes increasingly intrusive and bothersome.*

Courtney   SO WHAT DOES YOUR FAMILY THINK ABOUT IT??

Annie   THEY LOVE IT.

Sam   ABOUT WHAT??

Courtney   ABOUT THE BRAIN THING!

Annie   THEY LOVE IT!!

Sam   OH, YEAH, I DON'T KN –

Courtney   IT MUST BE REALLY HARD.

Annie   THEY LOVE IT!!!!!!!!!!!!!

(*to* **Sam**) ARE YOU HAVING A GOOD TIME?

Sam   YEAH, I'M HAVING A GREAT TIME.

Sam *shoves* **Annie,** *climbs onto the back plinths and sits. The scene switches to the basement with* **Chad.**

Chad (*high*)   Heyyyy, Sam, do you want one??

Sam   Yeah. Chad. Hit me.

Chad *passes a weed bong from the TV screen to* **Sam**. **Sam** *grabs it and takes a hit.*

Beat.

Chad   You know, don't take this the wrong way, but you're like way cooler with a brain aneurysm.

Sam *chokes from the smoke and coughs.*

Annie   No, Chad, you're way cooler with a brain aneurysm.

Sam   Thanks, Chad.

Sam *leaves, choking.*

Annie   Are you having a good time?

Sam   Yeah, I'm having a great time.

The scene switches back to the dance floor, now with **Laney.**

Laney   Hey Sam! So are you gonna do finals?

Sam   I don't know, Laney.

Annie   That's a good point, Laney.

Laney   Do you think you'll still graduate on time? Think you'll repeat the whole year? What does that mean financially?

Sam   I don't know, Laney.

Annie   Those are all good points, Laney.

Laney   What if you flunk the year? What does that mean for your future prospects? Are you getting back together with Brendan?

Sam   I don't know, Laney.

Annie   Eat glass, Laney.

(*concerned*) Are you still having a great time?

Sam   Yeah, I'm still having a great time!

The scene switches one last time into the bedroom with her final friend, **Jessie***.*

Jess (*sobbing*)   Hi Sam.

Sam   Oh god. What's wrong, Jessie?

Jessie   I'm sorr – S-am, it's just – it's so *scary* –

Sam   What's scary?

Jessie (*sobbing more*)   I just really don't want you to die.

Beat. **Sam** *doesn't know how to react. Meanwhile,* **Annie** *moves in close.*

Sam   . . . oh. Well, good thing I'm not really planning on it!

Annie   But if you do, do you really wanna spend one of your last nights on Earth doing this?

Sam (*ignoring*)   Hey, Jessie? Do you mind if I just go to the bathroom really quick?

Jessie (*sobbing even more*)   Oh my god – I've just u-upset y-you b-because I made th-this w-whole thing – ab-about me –

Sam   Oh, no! It's not, it's –

Jessie   Oh my god, I can't believe this happened on a night that I didn't wear waterproof mascara!

Sam   No, no, no, no, no! It's fine! It's fine! It's just –

Annie   – you're sucking the life out of me!

The scene suddenly switches to the bathroom as the two plop down. Exhausted.

Annie   Is this everything you hoped it would be?

Sam   Yeah, it's everything I hoped it would be.

Annie   Are you still having a good time?

Sam   Yeah, I'm still having a great time.

A knock on the door.

Paige   Hey, Sam, are you coming back out to the party??

Sam   Yeah, I'll be right there!!

Silence.

Annie   Do you wanna go home and talk about it?

Sam   Sure, Annie, let's go home and talk about it.

Annie *grins. The two get up and move to the center platform. Sounds re-enter from the party.*

Paige   Are you leaving?! Boo.

Courtney   Aw, Sam, Chad's gonna jump in the pool!

Chad   Sam, we're all gonna jump in the pool!

Paige   It's really important for her REM cycle she gets 9 hours of sleep.

Ester   Do you want to go to church in the morning?

Laney   Do you need paracetamol?

Jessie *(crying)*   I'm sorry guys, it's just that I'm really really scared –

All   Awww, Jessieeee, it's gonna be okayyy!!

Annie *and* **Sam** *return to the central platform. They say goodbye.*
Annie *nudges* **Sam**, *noticing someone in the distance.*
Sam *ignores her.*

Sam   Well . . . I almost did. But that was actually when I locked eyes with Nick for the first time that night.

Annie   I thought we were leaving?

Sam *(ignoring)*   When faced with a threat, or a *trauma*, the brain actually initiates a series of automatic responses designed to increase the individual's chances of survival.

It fundamentally gears itself towards self-preservation. So, after the initial adrenaline surge, it actually releases oxytocin – the 'bonding' or 'love hormone' – letting the logic part of the brain take a back seat and instinct take over and . . .

. . . Do you know when someone just sees you?

Sam *gently takes the camcorder and zooms in on the audience member designated as* **'Nick'***. The soundtrack to* High School Musical*'s 'Can I Have This Dance' begins to play.*

Annie   What happened to going home and talking about it?

Sam   Nick came over and asked me if I was okay. I couldn't speak. I couldn't find an answer.

Annie   The answer was no.

Sam   So he went and turned this song on the stereo, and –

Annie   Pretty sure that song was already playing, don't give him that much credit.

Sam   – it *doesn't matter*. Because at that moment, all that mattered is that we . . . began . . . to dance.

Sam *gestures to* **'Nick'** *to dance. Then winks.*

Sam (*whispering*)   Just kidding, you're not actually Nick. But can you hold this?

Sam *begins dancing with an imaginary* **Nick**. *Self-aware at first, joking for the benefit of the audience. Then slowly, caving into it. She completely loses herself in the memory of it.*

Sam   I know this was cheesy but . . . have you ever fallen in love with a human before?

Annie (*loudly*)   You weren't in love, Sam! You just wanted someone to –

Sam   FUCK OFF, Annie.

Annie *turns and stomps off-stage. Rummaging backstage is heard.*

Sam   I *looked* at him. And he *looked* at me. And I realized . . . I didn't have to be a superhero anymore, because someone else was going to save me.

One final beat.

A siren sounds.

All the lights go red.

The production shifts.

Suddenly, everyone is thrust inside of some sort of disturbing game show.

Scene 7. Game Show

Annie's *face takes over the projection and screens. Her voice becomes amplified off-stage. The voice of an over-the-top game show host.*

Host Annie HIYA EVERYBODY. Looks like we need to get Sam back on track, so we're going to play a game!! Welcome to The Best Game Show Ever!!!! Please welcome your host, Annie, Sam's aneurysm, aka the voice of reason she tries to pretend isn't there!

A musical intro plays. It's over-the-top, off-key, and way too long. **Annie** *comes out fully dressed now as a game show host.* **Sam** *gently places the camcorder back on its plinth.*

Sam (*pissed*) A game?

Annie A game!!

Sam On a game show???

Annie On a game show!!!

Sam (*furious*) Okay!!!!

Beat.

Sam & Annie (*to audience*) WELCOME TO THE GAME SHOW!!!

Musical sting. **Annie** *does a choreographed dance.* **Sam** *tries to keep up.*

Annie (*to audience*) On tonight's episode of 'Is She A Mess? Yes She Is!' where we give our contestants a healthy dose of reality and we're going to remind them of what?

Sam What?

Annie (*to audience*) Audience, when I say, 'Is She A Mess?' You say, 'Yes She Is!'

Ready?

. . . Is she a mess??!

The audience is given the chance to all shout back 'Yes, she is!'
Annie *moves to a new spotlight.* **Sam** *tries to keep up, but can't.*

Annie   Tonight's special guest is 20-year-old, bumbling
college student Sam. Introduce yourself, Sam.

Annie *holds out a mic.* **Sam** *snatches it.*

Sam   Hi, I'm Sam, what are your 20s for if not for
bumbling? I like mall, beach and of course, gorgeous –

Annie *sets off a BUZZER and grabs the mic back.*

Annie   That's enough, Sam! Audience, it's been 5 days and
Sam still hasn't thought about her new diagnosis . . .

Generated 'boo' sounds.

(*serious*) So, that brings us to round one –
DISTRACTIONS!!

Jeopardy boxes all come up on the scene with different categories.

Where do you want to start, Sam?

Sam (*annoyed*)   I'll take 'What is Boys' for $200, Annie.

Annie *reads the question revealed on the screen.*

Annie   Ooh. What really happened with Nick at the
party, Sam?

Sam   Well, Annie, I think Nick and I are both feeling good
about the situation. I think it's best to say that we're figuring
it out.

Annie   Hmm. Let's get Nick's opinion shall we?

A recording of **Annie** *dressed up and playing her version of 'Nick'
pops up on a screen.*

Annie as Nick   Uh. Well, I don't know, I'm actually feeling
really pressured by this situation.

Sam (*uncomfortable*) That's obviously not Nick. Next question. Boys for $400.

The box with $400 flips over on the screens.

Annie (*reading*) Are you gonna get back together with Brendan?

Sam Um, I think at this point in my life it's best to keep my options open.

Annie Interesting. Let's hear from Brendan!

A recording of **Annie** *dressed up as* **Brendan** *plays on the screen.*

Annie as Brendan Uh . . . Sam, you asked me to get back together right after the party?

Sam Okay, well, he's a really nice guy, guys.

Annie What she means by folks is that her mom loves him and she does not want to potentially die alone! Okay, audience, you know what to do . . . 'Is She A Mess???'

The audience is given the chance to respond 'Yes, she is!'. Another musical sting plays.

Sam (*loudly*) Well who wants to go to brain surgery alone! Next question! What is Internships for $800!

Annie Ooo, Sam's feeling spicy tonight.

The next question flips over.

(*reading*) What happened to the three interviews you had set up?

Sam (*confident*) Great question! They all went really well. They were super understanding about the whole situation and I think I'll be hearing from them all quite soon.

Annie Interesting! Let's hear what the friends have to say.

Sam *shakes her head desperately at* **Annie** *to stop. But, it's too late. The friends pop up on the screens.*

Courtney   The first one she cried.

Laney   Second one she shouted.

Paige   Third one she passed out.

Jessie (*overly sensitive*)   I think it was really brave, Sam.

Sam (*defensive*)   Well, what can I say, I've got a lot of range.

Annie   I don't think we'll be hearing from those jobs anytime soon!

Sam   Annie –!

Annie   Audience? You know what to do! . . . 'Is She A Mess'???

The audience shouts back 'Yes, She Is!'

Annie   Time for your favorite round. Round Two: THE MILLION-DOLLAR QUESTION.

A new game show takes over. Lifelines pops up on the screen in 'Who Wants to be a Millionaire' style and the big question appears with four options on the projection.

(reading the question) 'Are you going to get life-changing brain surgery?'

What's the correct answer, Sam? Is it:

A. Yes, and potentially die?

B. No, and potentially die?

C. Bury your head in the sand, and potentially die.

D. Get hit by a bus, and die. Potentially.

Sam   Nice try, Annie. I'll use a lifeline. 50/50.

The '50/50' lifeline disappears and options C and D vanish.

Annie   Oooo. Not ideal. So, what's it gonna be Sam?

Sam   I'll phone an expert.

The 'Phone An Expert' lifeline vanquishes.

Annie   Alright, let's get the doctor in to review some facts.

A phone call. The **Doc** *answers.*

Doc   Well. There's two options to consider moving forward, Sam. You can either choose to live with the aneurysm and we monitor it every six months to see if it grows any larger. Size doesn't determine whether or not it will go off. We've seen smaller ones set off way earlier.

Annie (*snickering*)   That's what she said.

Doc   You'll need to stay away from drugs, smoking, alcohol, or anything that raises your blood pressure because those can be risk factors. Do you play sports? You're definitely going to need to stop while you have it in there. The thing is – once they go off, there is only about a 1–2% chance of a person's survival. If we decide to go for surgery, there is another –

Sam *becomes physically uncomfortable.*

Sam   Okay, okay! I'll use phone a friend!

Annie   Who's it gonna be?

Sam   I'll call –

Annie   Dad!

Sam   No! Annie –

Dad *pops up on the screens.*

Dad   Well, I mean the facts speak for themselves, Sam. If we don't get this taken care of, then the risk of rupture is most likely going to happen in 3–5 years anyway. If you're lucky. I don't understand why you're waiting honey, you need to get the surgery.

Sam *shifts and struggles to stay in 'performance' mode.*

Sam   Okay, that's enough –

Annie   Mom, anything to add?

Sam   Annie, no –!

Mom *pops up on the TV screens.*

Mom   Um, honey I just – I don't know, I keep calling and I want to make sure you're okay but you've not been picking up. I think surgery is the smartest thing to do. I-I know it's gonna be hard. But I do think you're really lucky they found it.

Sam   That's enough, Ann –

BUZZER!

Annie   Ooo. You've run out of time, Sam. That brings us to Round Three: EXISTENTIAL DREAD.

The 'R' in Dread slowly drops in red blood on the screens as the scene shifts to the third and final game.

You have 20 seconds to answer all of life's most important questions, Sam. Are you ready?

Sam (*dryly*)   Ready.

Annie   Are you gonna go to Heaven?

Sam   Heaven is inside of us.

Annie   What if you flunk this semester?

Sam   Well, all the greats were college dropouts anyways.

Annie   Are you a good person?

Sam   Is anyone really a good person?

Annie   How do you feel about your carbon footprint?

Sam   I've got small, dainty feet.

Annie   Have you wasted your life?

Sam   I don't think wasting time is a wasted life.

Annie   What about health? Do you need to change your lifestyle?

Sam I'm a black belt in Pilates, I'll be fine.

Annie What will you do if you survive?

Sam I'll continue to thrive.

Annie What do you have to show for your life?

Sam A lot.

Annie Do you think people will remember you?

Sam Yes.

Annie Do you think you let your parents down?

Sam No.

Annie Have you lived a life worth living?

Sam Yes.

Annie Who will be there for Micah when you're gone?

Sam *hesitates.*

Who will be there for Micah when you're gone?

Sam *can't find the words.*

Who will be there for Micah when you're gone?

Sam Pass!

Annie Should you get the surgery, Sam?

Sam Pass.

Annie Should you get the surgery, Sam?

Sam Uh – Next question.

The family and friends' voices and videos begin to chime in again, creating a cacophony.

Annie Should you get the surgery, Sam?

Sam Yes.

Annie Should you get the surgery, Sam?

Sam   No.

Annie   Should you get the surgery, Sam?

Sam   I don't know.

Annie   Should you get the surgery, Sam?

Sam   Annie.

Annie   Should you get the surgery, Sam?

Sam   Stop.

Annie   Should you get the surgery, Sam?

Sam   Stop!

Annie   Should you get the surgery, Sam?

Sam   Stop! I said stop! I said stop! I SAID STOP!!!!

Sam *spins towards* **Annie**, *nearly taking a swing. Everything in the production stops.*

Lights come up. **Annie** *stares at* **Sam**, *then stalks off.*

Sam *tries to breathe and calm down. On the verge of a panic attack.*

A long silence.

Ka-Dink – Ka-Dink – Ka-Dink . . . **Micah** *pops up on all the screens. It throws* **Sam** *off.*

Micah   You should get the surgery, Sam.

Sam   Micah–stop–no. Stop –! I don't want to do this. Annie? Stop –

Micah   You will be okay.

Sam   Micah–no–you don't know that – Please–Annie–turn this off –. Stop. This isn't supposed to – I don't wanna –

Micah   You're Batman.

A small laugh escapes her. She looks down.

Sam   . . . Batman.

Silence.

Slowly, **Sam** *gets up and stands in the center of the platform. Determined to play along.*

So I did what any superhero would do . . . I went on spring break.

LMFAO'S 'SHOTS' starts playing immediately.

Annie *bursts back in dressed head-to-toe for Spring Break.*

Scene 8. Spring Break

Annie ALRIGHT LADIES AND GENTLEMEN, WHO'S READY TO GET FUCKED UP?

Music plays as **Annie** *shoots into the crowd. She pours shots, taunts, and plays games with willing audience members.* **Sam** *grabs a drink, stunned and lost. She protectively holds the camcorder.* **Annie** *notices and snatches it from* **Sam**. **Sam** *tries to resist but isn't quick enough.* **Sam** *takes a long drink and suddenly remembers where they are.*

Sam DRIVING. It takes my roommates and I 12 hours to get there. I take the night shift. Jessie's sitting in front with me but neither of us know what to say to each other. Pretty sure we've never had to spend this long in a confined space together. Paige has requested – nay, demanded – we keep the music to a strict volume of +1 to let the others in the back sleep. Instrumental only. We don't know what else to say to each other so we start talking about driving. How crazy it is. How crazy it is that we can travel at 80 miles per hour and how easy it would be to just kill everyone by the turn of a wheel. It's dark but we're bonding. Paige yells at us from the back. We laugh. I can see Jessie's tired and she doesn't really want to be awake so I tell her it's okay. She can sleep. I'm fine on my own. I'm *always* fine. She passes out. My eyes start getting a bit blurry. I think it's because I'm tired but I suddenly realize I'm crying. We'd all taken the philosophy of not mentioning she-who-must-not-be-named at all anymore. Ever, really. Had I known that first night was my only night to talk about my – Annie – I would have played my cards differently –

She points to **Annie** *in the crowd.*

Cheers, bitch. But now that'd passed and everyone had found their own ways of coping, which was – not to talk

about it at all anymore. I scheduled the surgery for 3 days
after Spring Break. Thoughts about it were looming
constantly. Every headache I had, every hangover, I was
worried something was wrong. My parents had kept calling.
I didn't answer. They all had some sort of unwarranted
advice, everyone had some sort of unwarranted advice.
And all I wanted to do was admit the truth.

Annie *gets up with the camcorder.*

I was sad, and lonely, and terrified of this bomb silently
ticking away inside my head.

Annie   Did you really think it was smart to be there, Sam???

Sam   We arrive at the motel to a display of complete
hedonism. From the parking lot to beach the place is packed
with underage debauchery . . . it's incredible.

Annie   Wowwww, that sounds incredibleeeee.

Sam   Paige and Courtney shoot off to a mob of half-naked
20-year-olds dancing by the beach. Jessie and Laney beeline
straight to the pool. And I head towards Nick. Things had
been weird ever since the party –

Annie   BORINGGGGG!!!

CLUB #1: Everything suddenly goes white as **Sam** *keels over from
a blinding headache. Scene jumps and a new song starts. Suddenly
we're inside a club.*

Annie   WHO WANTS SHOTS?!

Sam   Annie – what the hell are you –

Annie   Paige, Laney, Jessie, Courtney – All you bitches!!!!

*The friends all join on screens, decked out in Spring
Break gear.*

All (*screaming*)   YEAH! ME! ME! ME! ME! MEEEEE!!

Annie   Are you going to let everyone down, Sam?

Sam *looks at her and turns to the audience.*

Sam (*yelling*)   LET'S DO SHOTS!!!!!

Dance floor #1: The scene jumps and suddenly they're on a dance floor. **Annie** *dances with her cool moves, unbothered.* **Sam** *tries her hardest to copy and outdo* **Annie**.

Annie *throws a move her way. Suddenly,* **Sam** *gets a searing headache.* **Courtney** *pops up on a TV.*

Courtney (*drunk*)   Babeee, youuuu loook soo goooood!!!!

Sam (*searching*)   Courtney! Hey! Can we talk about my head?!!

Courtney (*from a different TV screen*)   Eww, don't go to bed!!!

Sam   No – my head!

Courtney (*from a different TV screen again*)   Lol, it's probably just a hangover!!! Let's get a drink!

Screens switch off. Back on the dance floor. **Annie** *suddenly has the camcorder again, recording* **Sam**.

Annie   She already had a drink, Sam . . . Seems like she didn't want to talk about your head.

Sam   Maybe she wanted two! Double parking is a thing!

Nick #1: **Sam** *snatches the camcorder as* **Annie** *spins her into a new scene.* **Nick**'*s there.*

Sam (*surprised*)   Nick . . . ! Hey. Can we ta –

Annie *switches the scene again before she can finish.* **Sam** *is jarred.*

Annie   Maybe you should slow down, Sam . . . You're looking sloppy out there.

Toilet #1: WHAM. Suddenly they're inside a toilet. It takes **Sam** *a moment to recover.*

Laney *pops up on a screen.*

Laney (*patronizing*)   Are you okay?

Sam   I don't know – Laney, I think there's something weird going on with Nick and I –

Annie   Yeah I'm sure that 'hey' really got his dick hard.

Laney   You should stay with Brendan, Sam. He's such a nice guy.

Toilet flushes.

Outside #1: The two face off as **Sam** *shoves* **Annie**. *Suddenly all the friends pop up.*

All   Oh there you are!! / Omg did you guys see Chad looking like a complete douchebag on the dance floor? / And Ester grinding on everyone? / So embarrassing.

Sam   Has anyone seen Nick?

All   Ugh, you're not still on that are you? / Move on, Sam, you're way better than him / He's such a douchebag / Fuck him, he's not good enough for you!

Sam   Yeah, hey guys, can we actually talk about –

Annie *snaps her fingers and* **Sam** *gets another searing headache. Everything goes white.*

Laney   Do you need ibuprofen, Sam?

Sam   Yeah, I mean no, it's just that my head –

Paige (*screaming*)   Oh my goddddddd!!

All   What's wrong?!

Paige   I just broke a nail!!

Courtney   Omg that's the worst!

Laney   Didn't you just get those done?!

Jessie   Those hurt so bad!

Paige   Ugh, I literally wanna die.

Courtney   We'll see you out there Sam!

They leave.

Annie   Dickheads.

Sam *ignores* **Annie**, *determined not to break.*

Club #2. Back at the club. **Sam** *aggressively takes the lead.*

Sam   WHO WANTS SHOTS?

NO I WAS NEXT, I WAS NEXT.

I WANT 4 SHOTS –

Annie   6 shots!!

Sam   6 SHOTS!!

Annie   Make 'em doubles!

Sam   Make 'em triples!!

Friends all chime in.

All   Lol, Sam, we don't need more / No let's go dance! /
I'll take one! / Let's do it!

Sam   No–You–you–you–you–you– . . . If we were all gonna
get fucked up –???

Sam/Annie   Then we'll get fucked up!!!

Dance #2. **Sam** *tries even harder to outdo* **Annie** *now.* **Annie**
starts doing the worm. **Sam** *tries doing the worm. Friends pop up
on various screens.*

Paige   I'm so glad we're not at school!

Sam   Paige! Babe, can we talk?!

Jessie (*crying/shouting*)   Guys, promise we'll never leave
each other –

Sam   Jessie! I need to –

Laney   We're going to remember this night forever!!

Sam   Laney, Courtney, can –

Courtney   This is our last chance to have fun before we're old and boring!!

Sam   I –

All   You're gonna be fine, Sam! Let's go do shots to celebrate!!

And before **Sam** *knows it, they're gone.* **Annie** *waits with an offer of a drink in her hand. Silently asking.* **Sam** *pauses. Then snatches the drink. Takes a huge gulp. She throws up as* **Annie** *spins her around again.*

Nick #2: *She holds her cup, throw-up seeping down her shirt.* **Nick** *stands opposite.*

Sam   Oh my god, no – Nick, it's fine it's just soup! Let's keep – good chat – one sec – I'll be back – !

Toilet #2: The production tilts sideways as **Sam** *and* **Annie** *both begin to throw up now.*

Sam *stays slumped over the toilet. Friends enter.*

Paige   Where are you, bitch??

Courtney (*disgusted*)   Did you just throw up on yourself?

Laney (*patronizing*)   I think you should probably go home.

Jessie (*crying*)   Should I call 911. Or maybe your mom?

Annie   SHUT UP WE'RE FINE.

Sam *and* **Annie** *drag their bodies up to the center.* **Annie** *holds the camera.*

Annie (*desperately*)   Are you having a good time?

Sam *swipes for the camera. Misses.*

Annie (*exhausted*)   Are you having a good time?

Sam *swipes again, misses.* **Annie** *grabs her hair and unwillingly thrusts* **Sam** *onto the platform.*

Blackout.

Then strobe lights come up.

Club #3: **Sam**, *alone, in the club going mad on a dance floor by herself.*

Sound cuts.

Spotlight #1. Lights come up on **Annie** *– USR.*

Annie (*worriedly*)   Are you having a good time?

Lights down.

Club #4: Strobe back up on **Sam**. *Still in the club. Still alone and nearly delirious.*

Sound cuts.

Spotlight #2. Lights come up on **Annie** *– DSL.*

Annie (*desperately*)   Are you having a good time?

Lights go down.

Club #5: Lights strobing. **Sam**, *still alone, starts to have a panic attack. She finds and rips her wet shirt off her body.*

Sound cuts.

Spotlight #3. Lights come up on **Annie** *– USL (Platform).*

Annie   Are you having a good time?

Lights go down.

Club #6: Strobes once more. **Sam** *stands completely still in a daze.*

Annie (*shouting*)   Are you having a good time?

The friends start popping up on the screens.

All   She's been going crazy recently / She's completely lost it / I'm worried / It's not our fault she won't talk about it / Guys we're on Spring Break are we gonna spend the whole time talking about Sam / She's gonna be fine, she just wants attention –

Doc *pops up on all the screens.*

Doc Just remember to stay away from things that could trigger it, Sam. Things like smoking, drinking, over-stimulation. Anything that's going to raise your blood pressure really –

Panic starts to rise. **Sam** *looks around.*

Sam Nick?

Nick!

Hey –

Has anyone seen –

Hey guys where's –

Hey, Ni –

Ni –

Hey –

Nick #3: *Sam stumbles off the platform, suddenly pulled into a memory with* **Nick.**

Music stops. But **Sam** *shouts above it as if it's still there.*

NICK!

(*shouting*) Hey – will you go home with me?

What? No, I can't hear you!

No, I'm asking you to go home with me!

No, no because my head hurts! And I'm – I just need to talk!!

I just need to TALK TO SOMEONE BECAUSE I'M SC – Look – I think you're in love with me – ! I think I'm in love with you – ! I know it's not the thing or whatever to say that but I just need us to talk – because then we can figure it all out. Because then it's all going to be – This isn't about the – the – About Annie. It's time! We were supposed to

have – I just thought I was supposed to have all this time –
all this time to – figure this – to figure everything out – I'm
supposed to have all this time to figure life out! And if you
just come with me – we can talk, we can make everything
okay – if you just come home with me. Please, Nick, if you
just come home with me and it will all be okay.

What?

Oh.

No . . .

Of course . . .

I'm sorry, I'm really so –

You totally sh –

She's really pretty, dude.

Beat.

Sam *stumbles backwards, starting to breathe heavily. She hits the
plinth. Falls.*

Looks around. Disoriented.

She notices the audience for the first time.

What are you all –

What is going –

She starts to panic. Tears rising. She looks around.

She notices **Annie**. **Annie** *holds the camcorder, recording.*

Sam *sees it.*

And explodes.

(*furious*) Why are you staring at me?

What are you looking at?

If I wanted a mom, I'd just call her Laney!

Why are you so interested, Paige?

You don't even care.

None of you even fucking care.

None of you even fucking care!

Hey everybody!! I'm gonna die on Monday and none of my friends even fucking care!!

Don't tell me to calm down you calm down you.

I'm fine. Okay? I said I'm fine.

Oh boo hoo, Jessie, why are you always crying –?

Don't tell me to shut up you shut up.

I said I'm fine! Okay?

Will everyone just shut the fuck up???

Okay? I said I'm fine!!

Will everyone please just SHUT UP!

I'M FINE.

I SAID I'M FINE.

I'M FUCKING FINE.

Silence.

Sam *laughs.*

Then cries.

Oh my god . . .

I'm gonna die on Monday, and you're all going to be completely fine without me.

Silence.

Sam's *chest heaves as a real panic attack starts to set in. She tries to shake it off.* **Annie** *gently comes over.*

Annie   Sam . . . I –

Sam   Get the fuck away from me.

Sam *grabs the camcorder and protectively moves it away from her.*
Phones start ringing.

Sam   What are you doing?

Mom's voice answers.

Mom (*Voicemail*)   Hi, you've reached Robin Ipema, please
leave a name and message at the beep!

Sam   Stop. Annie, don't. Please. Stop.

Another phone call. **Dad** *answers.*

Dad (*cutting out*)   Honey?? Honey, it's really loud out
there. I can't really hear you. It's 2am. Can I call you in
the morning?

Sam   Stop! Stop! Stop!! Why are you doing this to me?

Another phone rings. No answer. It rings again. No answer.
It rings again. **Sam** *desperately searches for a way to turn the*
show off.

Sam   Stop!

Annie   Sam . . . I – I'm so so –

Annie *opens her arms and tries to embrace* **Sam**. *The doctor starts*
glitching on the screens.

Doc   It's going to feel like – it's going to feel like – it's going
to feel like – it's going to feel like –

Sam (*terrified*)   Stop! Annie, why are you doing this? Please!
Stop! Please –

Both are crying now. **Sam** *approaches* **Annie** *on the platform.*
The two embrace.

Annie   Sam, I'm sorry, I'm sorry, I just wanted you to
admit that you needed –

Doc   It's going to feel like you've been hit by a truck.

Sam *headbutts* **Annie**.

They fight.

Sam *finds a television screen on set. Lifts it up . . . And knocks* **Annie** *out.*

Scene 9. Surgery

Suddenly, the production is thrust inside a surgical room. **Sam** *goes still. Realizing what she's done. She looks at the audience. Puts on a doctor's coat. And calmly continues.*

Sam There are a few things to consider when operating that may affect the outcome. Namely, where you decide to operate from. First, the patient will be asked a series of questions. Primarily to figure out what they value in life. Have a think about what you'd want to save. I didn't know – I just knew that I loved soccer. So we operated from the right side. To preserve motor functions.

She grabs a disinfectant wipe from her pocket.

First, the head is shaved and disinfected – Uh . . . Just so you know, this part is about to get very, very graphic. So if anyone here dislikes blood, has a phobia, or gets uncomfortable around medical stuff, I would highly suggest stepping out of the room for a moment. Otherwise, you can plug your ears or close your eyes. You're welcome to leave at any time, and we'll let you back in.

Audience members are given appropriate time and chance to leave the stage if they choose before she continues. **Sam** *is welcome to ad lib here to fill the time.*

Everyone ready?

Okay.

Let's begin.

The screens change to the outside of **Sam**'s *brain.*

First, the scalp is removed and a curve incision is made to expose the skull. Next, we drill.

A video of her surgery plays on the screens as **Sam** *performs the surgery on* **Annie**.

The next part is a tough membrane called the dura mater.
It can take a little work getting through. But once
you do –

Noise ends. The skull is removed.

– you finally expose the brain and you're in. Everyone get
comfortable because the next bit takes about 6–8 hours
of meticulous work with micro instruments, navigating
through the brain. By the way, we found out mid-operation
that my body burns through meds twice as quickly as an
average person. So half my recovery was without the help of
medication and what you're seeing, that's exactly what I felt.

*The brain tissue is cut, and the recording navigates through the
brain as* **Sam** *speaks.*

First, they peel back the brain tissue. Then, they navigate
through the brain's natural folds and cerebrospinal fluid
in order to create a pathway to the aneurysm. If you're even
a quarter of a millimetre off, you're fucked. Or you're dead.

Once they locate the aneurysm, they dissect the membranes
around it. Exposing the aneurysm's neck. They verify from
multiple angles, and then the moment of truth. Placing the
metal clip.

Sam *displays a small metal clip.*

It's basically a tiny paper clip used to cinch the aneurysm,
to stop the blood from flowing into the stretched area
anymore. Cutting it off.

She goes inside the TV head and carefully places the metal clip.

After the clip is placed, they ensure haemostasis, which
means that everything's working as it should be, and make
their way delicately out of the skull. The dura mater from
before is carefully sutured closed to protect the brain
tissue. Any bleeding is meticulously controlled to prevent
complications. The bone flap was placed back in the original
position and secured, with small plates and screws.

Sam *takes the TV head off* **Annie** *and places it back. Meanwhile,* **Annie** *tries to numbly escape.* **Sam** *watches.*

The patient is left in ICU recovery to be closely monitored. The next days and weeks are vital.

As **Annie** *tries to escape,* **Sam** *pulls each neuron cable from the TV plugs, cutting her off.* **Annie** *dies.* **Sam** *stands still for a moment. Then takes off the coat, and replaces it with the hospital gown. A recording of the doctor begins to play as she undresses and lies down, losing all function.*

Doc   You're young. Agile. You'll be being back up and running in no time. Well, maybe not running. But you get the gist.

Now, just to remember, possible risk factors and side effects that are likely to happen during recovery, which takes approximately 5–7 years.

-Blindness

-Stroke

-Nerve damage

-Seizures

-Nausea

-Fatigue

-Vomiting

-Cognitive impairments including:

    -Loss of motor functions

    -Speech, sense, and memory

    -Emotional and sleep disturbances

    -The inability to regulate bodily functions

    -Difficulties with memory, concentration, processing information, or decision-making . . .

-Bleeding

-Swelling

-Bruising

-Infection

Oh, yes, and even after all that still – death.

Sam *flops over. Unconscious.*

The lights go out.

Scene 10. Recovery

In the dark, single electric lightning bolts of neuron networks shoot across the space. Not quite connecting. Sounds and voices from the outside world come in a rumble like far-off thunder. The sequence continues, voices and noises getting louder and louder. Neurons widely shooting across trying to find connections, but can't. It subsides. **Sam** *drags herself to the TV. Turns it on. And a recording of her in a hospital gown plays.*

Recorded Sam   When the body re-learns how to walk, it has to reform completely new neural connections. Typically from a life-altering event, particularly a traumatic one, the brain works in overdrive to rewire around it. That's why the initial days of recovery, the first few days after the event, neural plasticity is at its highest and the rebuilding of the neural pathways then is vitally important if the patient is to make a full recovery. That's also when the brain has sustained the most trauma. Pain is stuck in overdrive. Memories play in jilted order. Malfunction happens as the brain attempts to reestablish disrupted connections.

As the recording plays, **Sam** *slides upright and prepares to try walking again.*

It's the same process we go through as a child, piecing things together. Only adults have a higher level of cognitive awareness about the process. So it can be emotionally distressing. For me, it was like continually falling off the edge of a cliff.

Sam *steps off, tries to stand. Suddenly the cacophony of noise, memories in jilted order flicker, neurons spiking off – plunged back into the dark.*

The key is resilience and patience. And you have to think about every action that you're doing. You have to think about pressing your wrist down. Then doing it. Think

about sliding your body upright. Then doing it.
Think about putting your foot on the ground. Then
doing it. Think about tensing your core. Then doing it.
Think about balancing. Then doing it. Think about lifting
your knee, stretching your leg, taking your first step.
Then do it.

As the recording explains the steps, **Sam** *follows them on the stage.*
Slips and tries again. Slips and tries again. A new recorded series
of her family recollecting the event begins to play as **Sam** *slowly*
recovers, fighting to plug back in the neuron cables.

Mom (*recollecting*)   I was just so worried about you. We
had no clue if you were going to be okay. It was just days of
waiting to find out. And you looked so – You just weren't
speaking – I think you were in so much pain that you
couldn't. And it was awful – it was the worst thing, sitting
there, not being able to help you.

Micah   Is she gonna be okay?

Mom   We don't know yet, bud, we just have to wait and see.

Micah   She will be . . . she's Batman.

Dad   It was after you got up and walked for the first time.
You only made it a few steps before you were done. And
we were all hovering around, congratulating you, worried
because we still didn't know if you were okay and you had
this look on your face. You were so mad and you just go.
'I'm fine. My head just hurts.' It's hard to explain the feeling.
We knew you were feeling miserable, but it was great to hear
because for us – that was the moment we knew you were
going to be okay. But for you, it was only just beginning.

Recorded Sam   I tried to go back to school afterwards.

But I couldn't sustain it.

I was miserable to be around at best.

My friends didn't know how to act.

They told me I'd changed.

Which was funny considering none of them had come to visit during the recovery.

Nick certainly didn't.

When my roommates finally did –

You could tell they didn't want to be there. I tried so hard to impress them – remind them that I was fun and funny and this would only be for a little while . . . that I ended up back in the hospital for 2 weeks. The Doc told my parents it had nearly killed me.

Sam *finally finishes and sits slumped on the central box. Exhausted. She pulls a balloon out of her bra. It's another soccer ball.*

But none of that mattered. All that mattered was that in 6 weeks I would start walking.

In 12, I would start running.

And in 6 months, I would be happy because I would be playing soccer.

She tries to blow it up. She can't. She tries harder and harder.

Doc   I'm so sorry, Sam, I thought you understood that. Even after a surgery like that, a brain aneurysm is still a risk to certain activities. It's not been removed, it only gets clipped. So it's something you'll have to be conscious of for the rest of your life. And I'm afraid soccer is going to be one of those things that's out of the picture.

(*Pause*)

You're alive, Sam.

You're one of the lucky ones.

Sam *gives up and clutches the balloon. She sits in the hospital. Looking outward. Either early morning or evening, not busy or loud in the hospital.*

Sam   I think . . .

(*beat*)

I think it was my . . .

(*beat*)

I think it was my . . . f.

(*beat*)

I'm tired.

(*beat*)

Because of my face.

(*beat*)

Am I?

(*beat*)

They stayed in the corner there.

They looked scared.

(*beat*)

Why didn't anyone come back?

(*beat*)

And Nick . . .

(*beat*)

I don't have any friends.

(*pause*)

I don't even know who I –

(*beat*)

I don't think I wanna be here, Dad.

(*beat*)

It's too hard.

No one likes me.

Dad *pops on the screen.*

Dad   That's not true Sam, we like you.

Sam (*rolls her eyes*)   Ugh. Dad! You're my dad! You have to like me.

Dad   That's not true. I have definitely had many *many* moments where I have not liked you.

Sam (*laughs*)   Okay.

Dad   Many.

Sam   Enough!

Dad   Just kidding.

I like the you that likes you.

Sam   Ugh, you're so cheesy Dad.

Pause.

Dad   Promise if you make it, you'll be whoever you want to be.

A long silence.

Sam *doesn't speak. She simply stands and takes in the messy set.*

She shuffles to the back.

She lifts the back curtain and places it on a clip.

Then another clip.

Then another.

She looks at the audience.

Sam   So I built a fort. And no one was allowed inside.

She leaves. Then comes back for a moment.

Sam Except for Micah.

She smiles and disappears inside the fort.

A video game begins to play as a projection of the two of them: one real, and one imagined, begins to play out.

Sam Go to your left – good! Now over there.

Micah – no. Not there, that's me.

Micah! Stop! No – ! Micah, that's me – that's me! Micah!!

Explosion on the video game.

Micah (*giggles*) Got you!

Sam (*semi-joking*) Micah. Stop it. I'm not going to play with you if you keep killing me.

Sound of the game playing again . . . and another explosion.

Sam Micah stop! Don't . . . alright. I told you, I'm done.

Micah Sheesh.

Sam What?

Micah You are grumpy.

Sam No I'm not. You just keep killing me. Be nice.

Micah I am nice. You are not nice.

Sam (*getting upset*) Micah! Why would you say that? Don't say that.

Micah You're no fun.

Sam Micah. Stop.

Micah I don't want to play with you.

(**Sam** *starts to cry*)

Micah You're upset / Are you sad?

Sam No I'm fine, let's just play.

Micah   Are you okay?

Sam   Micah, I'm fine, I – my head just hurts. I'm fine. I just have a headache.

Micah   What is a headache?

Sam   You know what a headache is, bud.

Micah   No, I don't.

Sam *groans, exhausted and has a headache now.*

Sam   A headache is when your head is like really full and you're frustrated because no one can see it but it hurts. That's what a headache is.

Micah   Oh.

Sam   Yeah.

Micah   That is really hard.

Sam   Yeah. It is hard.

Micah   It's okay. You're Batman.

Sam   Micah, Batman's not – I don't feel like Batman anymore.

Micah   You are Batman to me.

Sam   Thanks.

Micah   I love you, Sam.

Sam   I love you too, Robin.

Micah   Who's Robin?

Slowly from behind the fort in the projection, **Sam** *turns the camera and flips it to record herself. Her face live-streams on all of the TVs.*

Sam (*wiping tears*)   So, I did what any superhero would do, and I started to – (*catching*) Sorry.

I started to –

I started to pick up the –

Well . . .

I – . . . I actually just started to cry.

(*small laugh*) For weeks.

That was all I did.

I just . . .

Cried.

A beat. She cries softly. It all comes tumbling out.

And then I started picking up the pieces and live my life.

But that was only because I had to.

Because I had this googly-eyed little –

And then I went back to school and I tried –

But I was just –

And my friends were –

And everything had just –

Changed.

I had just – changed.

A phone call rings. She pauses. Clears her throat. Tries to start again.

Sorry. I – . . . um –

Another phone call rings.

Sorry that's um . . . that's really distracting, I uh –

A phone call starts.

Sorry, I –

Another ring. Another ring, another ring, until eventually . . .

Nurse Hi Sam, this is Nurse Jackson from Metro Health Hospital. We . . . We're so sorry . . . took a look at your new scan and . . . I don't know how to tell you this. We found something again. We need you to come back as soon as possible. We think that we found another spot again.

Sam *re-enters from the door. She sits and watches and rewinds the images playing on stage. Rewinding. Watching. Rewinding. Watching. Rewinding. Watching. Until eventually . . . she presses 'Pause'.*

Sam   Did you know that the brain tells us stories . . . fills in the gaps in our memories . . . to put together a collection of moments into a cohesive narrative . . . We do it for survival. To make sense of the past. In order to predict the future. To inform the present moment.

And I could – I could spend a lifetime rewinding the past to try to make sense of why this all happened here . . .

But the truth is . . . that even though we have 86 billion neurons. Even though our brains can create these fantastic stories about why something happens to us . . . sometimes, life just makes no sense.

And as much as I wish my aneurysm was a beautiful red-haired Scottish woman . . . it's not. And as much as I wish this part of the story wasn't true, it is. And every 12 months I go in, I get a scan to see if it gets bigger.

And I don't have any brain or science facts to tell you that sometimes . . . it's just hard.

But, I do know this.

She steps onto the platform and flips the camcorder back on, pressing 'record'.

There are these moments in life where you can look around and see it. Your life. What's ahead of you, behind you, and you . . . in the middle of it. With a choice to make. And I think these moments are beautiful. Terrifying. Confusing. But beautiful. And this is what I choose to do.

I'm going to lift my knee, stretch my leg, and keep taking my next step.

As she flips the camcorder off **Annie** *pops up one final time on the screens.*

Annie (*off-stage*)   *Blackout.*

The production fades to black.

End of play.

Discover. Read. Listen. Watch.

A NEW WAY TO ENGAGE WITH PLAYS

This award-winning digital library features over 3,000 playtexts, 400 audio plays, 300 hours of video and 360 scholarly books.

Playtexts published by Methuen Drama, The Arden Shakespeare, Faber & Faber, Playwrights Canada Press, Aurora Metro Books and Nick Hern Books.

Audio Plays from L.A. Theatre Works featuring classic and modern works from the oeuvres of leading American playwrights.

Video collections including films of live performances from the RSC, The Globe and The National Theatre, as well as acting masterclasses and BBC feature films and documentaries.

FIND OUT MORE:
www.dramaonlinelibrary.com • 🐦 @dramaonlinelib

Methuen Drama Modern Plays

include

Bola Agbaje
Edward Albee
Ayad Akhtar
Jean Anouilh
John Arden
Peter Barnes
Sebastian Barry
Clare Barron
Alistair Beaton
Brendan Behan
Edward Bond
William Boyd
Bertolt Brecht
Howard Brenton
Amelia Bullmore
Anthony Burgess
Leo Butler
Jim Cartwright
Lolita Chakrabarti
Caryl Churchill
Lucinda Coxon
Tim Crouch
Shelagh Delaney
Ishy Din
Claire Dowie
David Edgar
David Eldridge
Dario Fo
Michael Frayn
John Godber
James Graham
David Greig
John Guare
Lauren Gunderson
Peter Handke
David Harrower
Jonathan Harvey
Robert Holman
David Ireland
Sarah Kane

Barrie Keeffe
Jasmine Lee-Jones
Anders Lustgarten
Duncan Macmillan
David Mamet
Patrick Marber
Martin McDonagh
Arthur Miller
Alistair McDowall
Tom Murphy
Phyllis Nagy
Anthony Neilson
Peter Nichols
Ben Okri
Joe Orton
Vinay Patel
Joe Penhall
Luigi Pirandello
Stephen Poliakoff
Lucy Prebble
Peter Quilter
Mark Ravenhill
Philip Ridley
Willy Russell
Jackie Sibblies Drury
Sam Shepard
Martin Sherman
Chris Shinn
Wole Soyinka
Simon Stephens
Kae Tempest
Anne Washburn
Laura Wade
Theatre Workshop
Timberlake Wertenbaker
Roy Williams
Snoo Wilson
Frances Ya-Chu Cowhig
Benjamin Zephaniah

Methuen Drama Contemporary Dramatists

include

John Arden (two volumes)
Arden & D'Arcy
Peter Barnes (three volumes)
Sebastian Barry
Mike Bartlett
Clare Barron
Brad Birch
Dermot Bolger
Edward Bond (ten volumes)
Howard Brenton (two volumes)
Leo Butler (two volumes)
Richard Cameron
Jim Cartwright
Caryl Churchill (two volumes)
Complicite
Sarah Daniels (two volumes)
Nick Darke
David Edgar (three volumes)
David Eldridge (two volumes)
Ben Elton
Per Olov Enquist
Dario Fo (two volumes)
Michael Frayn (four volumes)
John Godber (four volumes)
Paul Godfrey
James Graham (two volumes)
David Greig
John Guare
Lee Hall (two volumes)
Katori Hall
Peter Handke
Jonathan Harvey (two volumes)
Iain Heggie
Israel Horovitz
Declan Hughes
Terry Johnson (three volumes)
Sarah Kane
Barrie Keeffe
Bernard-Marie Koltès (two volumes)
Franz Xaver Kroetz
Kwame Kwei-Armah
David Lan
Bryony Lavery
Deborah Levy
Doug Lucie

Alistair MacDowall
Sabrina Mahfouz
David Mamet (six volumes)
Patrick Marber
Martin McDonagh
Duncan McLean
David Mercer (two volumes)
Anthony Minghella (two volumes)
Rory Mullarkey
Tom Murphy (six volumes)
Phyllis Nagy
Anthony Neilson (three volumes)
Peter Nichol (two volumes)
Philip Osment
Gary Owen
Louise Page
Stewart Parker (two volumes)
Joe Penhall (two volumes)
Stephen Poliakoff (three volumes)
David Rabe (two volumes)
Mark Ravenhill (three volumes)
Christina Reid
Philip Ridley (two volumes)
Willy Russell
Eric-Emmanuel Schmitt
Ntozake Shange
Sam Shepard (two volumes)
Martin Sherman (two volumes)
Christopher Shinn (two volumes)
Joshua Sobel
Wole Soyinka (two volumes)
Simon Stephens (five volumes)
Shelagh Stephenson
David Storey (three volumes)
C. P. Taylor
Sue Townsend
Judy Upton (two volumes)
Michel Vinaver (two volumes)
Arnold Wesker (two volumes)
Peter Whelan
Michael Wilcox
Roy Williams (four volumes)
David Williamson
Snoo Wilson (two volumes)
David Wood (two volumes)
Victoria Wood

For a complete listing of
Methuen Drama titles, visit:
www.bloomsbury.com/drama

Follow us on Twitter and keep up to date
with our news and publications
@MethuenDrama